HENRY J. BRUTON

The Promise of Peace: Economic Cooperation between Egypt and Israel

A Staff Paper

THE BROOKINGS INSTITUTION
Washington, D.C.

The Promise of Peace:
Economic Cooperation
between
Egypt and Israel

HENRY J. BRUTON

The Promise of Peace: Economic Cooperation between Egypt and Israel

A Staff Paper

THE BROOKINGS INSTITUTION
Washington, D.C.

Library of Congress Cataloging in Publication data:

Bruton, Henry J
  The promise of peace.
  "A staff paper."
  1. Egypt—Foreign economic relations—Israel.
  2. Israel—Foreign economic relations—Egypt. 3. Egypt—
Economic conditions—1952– . 4. Israel—Economic
conditions. I. Brookings Institution, Washington, D.C.
II. Title.
HF1611.7.Z4I752   337.5694062   80-70449
ISBN 0-8157-1125-5

1 2 3 4 5 6 7 8 9

THE BROOKINGS INSTITUTION is an independent organization devoted to nonpartisan research, education, and publication in economics, government, foreign policy, and the social sciences generally. Its principal purposes are to aid in the development of sound public policies and to promote public understanding of issues of national importance.

The Institution was founded on December 8, 1927, to merge the activities of the Institute for Government Research, founded in 1916, the Institute of Economics, founded in 1922, and the Robert Brookings Graduate School of Economics and Government, founded in 1924.

The Board of Trustees is responsible for the general administration of the Institution, while the immediate direction of the policies, program, and staff is vested in the President, assisted by an advisory committee of the officers and staff. The by-laws of the Institution state: "It is the function of the Trustees to make possible the conduct of scientific research, and publication, under the most favorable conditions, and to safeguard the independence of the research staff in the pursuit of their studies and in the publication of the results of such studies. It is not a part of their function to determine, control, or influence the conduct of particular investigations or the conclusions reached."

The President bears final responsibility for the decision to publish a manuscript as a Brookings book. In reaching his judgment on the competence, accuracy, and objectivity of each study, the President is advised by the director of the appropriate research program and weighs the views of a panel of expert outside readers who report to him in confidence on the quality of the work. Publication of a work signifies that it is deemed a competent treatment worthy of public consideration but does not imply endorsement of conclusions or recommendations.

The Institution maintains its position of neutrality on issues of public policy in order to safeguard the intellectual freedom of the staff. Hence interpretations or conclusions in Brookings publications should be understood to be solely those of the authors and should not be attributed to the Institution, to its trustees, officers, or other staff members, or to the organizations that support its research.

Foreword

THE PEACE negotiations between Israel and Egypt initiated by President Sadat's visit to Israel in 1977 constitute one of the great events of the last quarter-century. Though genuine peace is not yet at hand, it is appropriate to begin to examine some of the benefits that might flow from a lasting settlement of Israeli-Egyptian differences. In this staff paper, Henry J. Bruton reviews the problems and opportunities for economic cooperation that a secure peace may offer. He also considers how the United States might contribute to fostering such cooperation.

Suitable forms of cooperation between Egypt and Israel are not easy to discern because the two countries had never dealt with each other before President Sadat's visit to Israel in 1977. It is thus not possible to seek to restore or build from what once was. The problem is to find ways of beginning and nurturing cooperation.

Although the two economies differ greatly, they are similar in at least two important respects: both face economic problems of roughly the same kinds, and both have roughly the same opportunities for increasing economic welfare. From this Bruton infers that it is around the search for ways to meet these problems and to realize these opportunities that cooperation can evolve. He argues that direct cooperation between the two countries is needed more than aid programs, and he believes it important to try to establish strong informal links between small-scale industrial and agricultural entrepreneurs and workers in the two countries. Such links—resulting from visits, seminars, and so on—avoid some of the position-taking that often impedes the formal pursuit of cooperative goals by high-ranking government officials. Also, small-scale manufacturing and agriculture offer great potential for resolving many of the problems confronting each country. Bruton suggests that the United States can support these efforts by limited contributions of money and talent, but he believes that a large-scale, wide-ranging effort by the United States is not appropriate.

The author is professor of economics at Williams College and an economic consultant to the government of Egypt. He is indebted to Paul Clark, Richard Eckaus, and Seev Hirsch for their comments on drafts of this paper.

Bruton's work was supported by a grant from the Ford Foundation. The views expressed here are those of the author and should not be ascribed to the Ford Foundation or to the trustees, officers, or other staff members of the Brookings Institution.

BRUCE K. MAC LAURY
President

November 1980
Washington, D.C.

The Promise of Peace: Economic Cooperation between Egypt and Israel

ECONOMIC COOPERATION between Israel and Egypt presents many difficulties and offers many opportunities. That this is so scarcely needs documentation. The difficulties arise from the long period of hostilities between the two countries and the deep-seated differences between Arab and Jew manifest in virtually every aspect of social and cultural life and organization. Equally evident are the opportunities. Innumerable benefits for both nations can flow from reducing tension, from redirecting the energy and the initiative of leaders away from the issues of war toward those of economic and social welfare, and from reallocating labor and capital and foreign exchange from the war effort to economic improvement.

My purpose here is to examine the difficulties and opportunities for economic cooperation between Egypt and Israel and to consider the role that the United States might play in encouraging and developing such cooperation. My general theme is that cooperation, like peace itself, is delicate. To proceed slowly and surely with what is easy and obvious is to lay a foundation from which more difficult and complex problems may be tackled. Cooperation cannot be forced, but it is likely to emerge and grow with careful nurture.

Economic Similarities and Differences

The Egyptian and Israeli economies have important similarities and equally important differences. One difference, which should be noted at

1

the outset because it affects much of what follows, has to do with age and heritage. The Egyptian economy is part of one of the most ancient societies of the world. It has traditions and practices and institutional arrangements rooted in the far distant past. Roots, especially deep ones, affect not only how an economy functions, but also how it accepts change, how it reacts to new developments and policies, and the extent to which it is receptive to change and responsive to new opportunities. Roots also can provide strength and understanding; they help give direction, form, and hence meaning to economic change.

Israel, in contrast, is a young country. While a growing proportion of it is native born, the Israeli population is dominated by immigrants. This fact adds to the fluidity of the economy and of the society in general. Such a population also contributes to greater diversity of attitudes and values than that found in societies with little immigration and a fairly homogeneous population. In recent years a significant proportion of immigrants into Israel have been from Arab countries. Their native language is Arabic, and their life-style is more akin to that of Islam than to that of European and American Jewish communities. Immigrants from the West often speak little Hebrew and have trouble acclimating to a Middle Eastern land. Hence heterogeneity and diversity seem to be increasing. The binding force of Israeli society is basically the need to create and maintain a nation in an environment that has so far been inhospitable.

The Egyptian and Israeli economies have one dominant feature in common: they are under siege. Since the 1967 war, military expenditures have amounted to from 25 percent to 35 percent and possibly more of the gross domestic product. Even with very large amounts of aid and loans from abroad, the allocation of this proportion of resources to nonproductive uses has exerted enormous pressures on both economies. These pressures have in turn produced the expected results: government deficits, inflation, balance-of-payments and exchange-rate difficulties, and investment and capital allocation and maintenance problems. As the heavy military expenditures continued year after year, these problems became increasingly severe, and the tasks of economic management increasingly complex.

These characteristics affect how the two countries approach economic development and how their economies perform and are managed. They also affect the extent and content of the cooperation that can be expected between them.

Several more specific characteristics appear relevant to understanding the ways in which the two countries might cooperate. Accurate and up-to-date data are hard to come by, and a detailed quantitative survey has not been attempted. The data referred to in the following pages are, unless otherwise noted, from various World Bank data collections.

Population

Egypt's population of some 40 million is more than ten times that of Israel. Of Israel's population of fewer than four million, about 85 percent are Jews. (Data on Israel presented here do not pertain to areas now occupied by Israel beyond its 1967 borders.) Immigrants constitute a bit less than one-half of the Jewish population; of those born in Israel only about 20 percent or so are second-generation. Immigration has declined in recent years, while emigration has apparently increased. Projections of recent net immigration rates and the birthrates of Jews and Arabs to the year 2000 yield a population in Israel in that year about half Arab and half Jew, although some evidence indicates that the birthrate among Arabs is declining.

Egypt's population is much more homogeneous, and it is increasing at about 2.5 percent per year, entirely by natural propagation rather than immigration. About 90 percent of the population is Moslem. Egypt is almost fifty times larger in area than Israel, but virtually all 40 million Egyptians live along the Nile in an area less than twice that of Israel.

Gross Domestic Product

The Israeli gross domestic product per capita is about equal to that of the United Kingdom and from ten to twelve times that of Egypt. Egypt ranks in the lower third of the nations of the world.

In the 1950s and 1960s Israel's gross domestic product grew strongly, owing to an unusually high investment rate made possible by large capital transfers (mainly from the United States) combined with the rapid influx of skilled, aggressive labor. As military expenditures increased after 1967 at the expense of investment and as the flow of immigrants (particularly highly skilled ones) declined, the growth rate fell. It is probably correct to say that growth became more costly, in the sense that a given rate of investment produced a smaller increase in capacity in the mid-1970s than in the 1950s and 1960s. Preliminary data for 1977 and 1978 show very little real growth and an absolute decline in real investment.

Egypt's growth record during the 1950s and 1960s was less impressive than that of Israel. Investment rates were modest. In general they were somewhat below the rates attained by other countries with about the same per capita income. The early 1960s were the most favorable, but the real pinch came after 1967. Investment in constant prices in 1973 had not recovered to its 1965 level. Investment almost doubled between 1974 and 1975; it has remained fairly strong since. Growth over the past four or five years may have averaged close to 10 percent, though some evidence implies that this figure is unrealistically high. Much recent investment has been heavily concentrated, however, and a great deal of the existing capital stock seems not to have been well maintained. Net investment, therefore, is probably markedly below the gross figure. In agriculture, waterlogging and salination of arable land have often meant that sizeable investments are necessary simply to maintain current levels of output. Infrastructure and housing also show evidence of lack of full maintenance.

While difficulties with the investment rate are the most obvious factor accounting for Egypt's modest growth, other matters are also relevant. In particular, Egypt did not enjoy the advantages of the inflow of highly skilled, aggressive labor with strong links to world markets. The low investment rate in combination with a less well-trained labor force also meant that new, increasingly productive technology was slow in appearing. The nationalization of industries and various other measures followed in this period imposed severe management problems on government officials, some of whom were inexperienced. For all these reasons, growth was difficult to sustain.

Balance of Payments and Exchange Rate

Israel throughout its history and Egypt after 1967 (and especially after 1973) have received very large foreign loans and grants relative to the size of their economies. Imports of capital make possible deficits on current account, and both countries have had large (by international standards) deficits in recent years. The deficits shown in published tables probably understate the actual deficits, because some of the aid and loans associated with the importation of military hardware are not included.

Despite the capital influx, foreign exchange has been a major constraint in both countries over the last dozen years or so. It is also worth emphasizing that the capital imports were not large enough to relieve either country completely of the burdens of the military effort. Much of the capital that came into each country was used for military purposes, which has meant that nonmilitary production and consumption would have had to be reduced significantly if the capital influx had not continued. To put the same point differently, neither country became less dependent on foreign assistance in the 1970s. Hence each remains vulnerable to a reduction in capital flow.

Managing foreign accounts continues to be a hard task in both countries. Until recently, Egypt maintained an exchange rate that greatly undervalued foreign exchange and relied on import controls and the direct allocation of available foreign exchange by an allocation committee to limit demand. The Egyptian pound has now been devalued to a level more nearly consistent with the cost of earning foreign exchange, and import controls have been gradually relaxed. Even so, foreign exchange management continues to be of great concern to the government, and the allocation of imports to people and activities remains a strong influence on economic performance.

Israel has devalued frequently, largely to offset the effects of domestic inflation. Current account transactions are largely unrestricted, but capital movements are controlled.

Foreign exchange management is further complicated by the existence in both countries of an external debt that exceeds 75 percent of gross domestic product, possibly by a substantial amount. Debt service may amount to as much as 20 percent of exports in both countries. Egypt's situation is further complicated by its large debt repayment obligations to the USSR. Until 1979 as much as one-half of the value of Egyptian exports (chiefly cotton) have gone to the USSR, but very few imports have been received from that country. Trade with the USSR has been markedly reduced in recent years.

In Israel and Egypt, as in so many other developing countries, the effort to live with a precarious balance of payments has greatly distorted the allocation and use of resources.

Egypt's foreign exchange earnings took a significant turn in the latter part of 1979. In that period oil replaced raw cotton as the principal export. Also, remittances by Egyptian workers abroad are now very large, and Suez Canal receipts are growing as the canal becomes able to take larger ships. Tourism is somewhat uncertain owing to political problems, but long-run revenue prospects are generally favorable. These sources of strength of the balance of payments are, however, independent of developments in the main parts of the Egyptian economy. Exports other than oil have been falling in recent years, and there is little prospect that the trend will be reversed soon. The decline is a consequence of many factors, among which agricultural pricing policies and the retention of large domestic supplies are perhaps the most important. Egypt's imports are dominated by food grains. Imports of food grains and edible oils have been large and rising in recent years, and they claim a large share of foreign exchange earnings and aid.

Israel's exports are more diversified than Egypt's, but export growth in recent years has been modest. Fruits and vegetables are the largest single category of exports, but chemicals and electronics have been expanding in recent years. Textiles, iron and steel, and machinery are also important. Worked diamonds have constituted the largest single export category for some time; but since the rough diamonds are all imported, net exports in this sector are usually not as large as the other items just noted. Employment in the diamond-cutting sector is low and heavily concentrated among immigrants from Holland and Belgium.

Before 1973 Israel's largest import category was capital goods of all kinds. Now crude oil is by far the largest and will doubtless become even larger. Israeli oil imports and Egyptian imports of food grains and edible oils have similar economic effects although petroleum price increases have greatly exceeded those of food grains and edible oils.

The heavy dependence of Israel and Egypt on large capital inflows will continue for some time, even if relations between the two countries improve substantially. Both countries continue to seek stronger and longer-term commitments for foreign capital and aid, but it is not likely that any such commitments will be firm enough to reduce the present vulnerability to any great extent.

Inflation

Prices in both countries have increased rapidly in the recent past. Inflation in Israel is more open, and the price indexes now show increases of over 100 percent per year, and the rate seems to be accelerating. These increases have occurred despite extremely heavy taxation. The Israeli wage system is indexed to a considerable extent, but not enough to offset all the various costs of the inflation. Food subsidies and other subsidies—although being reduced—also help to reduce the full impact of inflation. In Egypt, price indexes probably do not reflect the full extent of inflation because many prices are legally controlled. Moreover, government stores often sell a fairly wide range of commodities at prices that represent a substantial subsidy. Even so, price indexes for the early months of 1980 showed a strongly rising trend, and there is little doubt that, as of mid-1980, inflation in Egypt was also accelerating. The efforts in both countries to cushion the effects of inflation, through subsidies and other means, has added to government borrowing needs and hence to inflationary pressure.

Inflation has also affected the distribution of income, although it is difficult to say exactly how. The distribution effect in Egypt is especially unclear because the effect of taxes is unclear. Given the great burden of military expenditures and the massive inflows of capital into both countries, preventing inflation from affecting the distribution of income, like preventing inflation itself, is essentially impossible.

Labor Force and Employment

The notions of unemployment and employment are difficult to apply to Egypt. There is little open unemployment, but the productivity of a large part of the labor force is very low indeed. The employment problem is equivalent to, or at least a big component of, the general problem of economic development in Egypt. In Israel employment presents a problem more familiar to western-trained economists. Survey data in recent years suggest that from 3.5 to 4.5 percent of the labor force is unemployed in the customary meaning of the term. This is small by most criteria, but in a small economy it is large enough to be of concern. Listed job vacancies in Israel usually exceed the number classified as unemployed. In both countries government employment is excessive: the work actually done could be done by considerably fewer people. The same problem is especially evident in Egypt. The Israeli employment problem appears to be growing more complex as the number of skilled immigrants suited for the kind of jobs now available declines.

In relation to possibilities for Israeli-Egyptian cooperation, the extent of employment and unemployment in either country is less important than various other characteristics of the labor force. The ratio of labor force to population is around one-quarter in Egypt and one-third in Israel. The difference is due in part to the different age distributions and to the much greater participation of women in the Israeli labor force. The different age distribution is, in turn, dependent on differing birthrates. About one-third of Israel's population is below 15 years of age, whereas 45 percent of Egypt's 40 million people are below 15. Such a difference has implications for investment allocation, consumption and saving rates, and availability of skills, among other things.

As already noted, half of the Israeli labor force is made up of immigrants. Israel has thus obtained a great many workers without incurring the cost of elementary education, although considerable practical training has been necessary. Israel is one of the few developing countries that has welcomed immigrants into positions of responsibility without hesitation. The aggressiveness, willingness to accept risk, and accumulated experience characteristic of many immigrants have been given free rein in Israel.

In contrast, the Egyptian labor force includes few immigrants. Roughly one of every ten members now works abroad, mainly in the Persian Gulf region. Egyptians, particularly schoolteachers, have long worked in the Gulf countries, but after 1973 their numbers increased substantially. They now include both semiskilled construction workers and unskilled laborers. The flow of Egyptian workers to the Gulf area is induced by wages ten or more times those in Egypt and the foreign exchange they send back is of great importance to Egypt. Yet the availability of such employment opportunities raises difficult policy questions. Electricians, plumbers, masons, and other skilled workers with maturity, experience, self-confidence and established position, who are badly needed at home, go abroad. The term "brain-drain" communicates something of the nature of the problem, but it is more than simply the outflow of people with valuable skills acquired at Egypt's expense. The outflow creates a vacuum that detrimentally affects what can be done at home and how it can be done.

Economic Structure and Management

Egypt is primarily an agricultural economy. The Nile delta includes some of the most intensively farmed land in the world. Methods are both primitive and ingenious. Yields are higher than world yields in general, but lower than other areas in which irrigation is relied on completely. Fertilizer is used less extensively than it is in many other countries. Only about 30 percent of Egypt's gross domestic product is of agricultural origin, but at least one-half of the labor force is engaged in agriculture. Service expenditures generate about 40 percent of gross domestic product and manufacturing about 20 percent. These percentages have not changed much over the last decade or more. Textiles are the principal manufacturing activity, employing about a quarter of a million workers, or something less than 20 percent of total manufacturing employment. This activity has great potential in Egypt, but the realization of that potential requires extensive rehabilitation of plant and equipment and updated management techniques. There is also a steel complex, an automobile assembly plant, aluminum plants, and fertilizer factories—all of significant size. Studies by Hansen and Nashashibi show, however, that many Egyptian industries, especially the newer ones, are "efficient" only at exchange rates much less favorable to Egypt than those that have prevailed in recent years.

Egyptian industry was nationalized in the early 1960s. All large-scale manufacturing activity is now owned or controlled by the government. All large banks, insurance companies, and other large financial institutions are government-owned and -operated. Some discussion of the sale of government-owned enterprises to private interests has been reported, but little has happened so far. Small enterprises account for about one-half of manufacturing employment, but for a much smaller proportion of output.

Agriculture is privately owned and operated, but government controls and regulations directly and extensively influence almost all decisions farmers make.

Market prices play a very modest role in allocative and distributive decisions in Egypt. The government relies heavily on direct controls and regulations to achieve its economic objectives. Controls take a variety of forms and have consequences difficult to trace. As the pressure on the economy has built up and continued, the task of managing the economy and its controls has become increasingly difficult. The "Open Door Policy" announced in 1974 has as one of its objectives a greater reliance on a market mechanism. Progress in this direction has been slow, but the intent seems to be to move gradually toward a wider role for the market.

Israel's economic structure more nearly resembles that of a Western European country. Less than 10 percent of Israel's gross domestic product is of agricultural origin, and an even smaller proportion of the labor force is engaged in agriculture. About one-half of gross domestic product originates in the services sector and the remainder in the industrial sector. Agriculture, though a small economic sector, is of great relevance to cooperation with Egypt for reasons explained below. Israel's imports and exports of agricultural products are about equal; the main food items imported now are cereals, meat, oils, and fats. The Israelis have also had considerable success with beef cattle despite the rather inhospitable environment, and with poultry.

Manufacturing growth has been rapid, especially from 1968 to 1975. It has been concentrated in electronics, transport, electrical machinery, and metals. Israel, like Egypt, has many small enterprises that cover virtually the entire range of manufacturing output.

The Israeli economy is more Western than Middle Eastern. An important part of the labor force was trained in the West, and all large enterprises have roots and links there. Technology and economic organization also resemble those in the West more than those in other Middle Eastern countries. The government is heavily involved almost throughout the economy. It designs, carries out, and manages the irrigation, afforestation, and construction projects that have been so important in Israel's development. It owns the largest manufacturing enterprises, and exercises considerable control over all others in allocating subsidized capital. The private sector is also very tightly controlled and directed by a great array of laws and regulations. The Israeli approach to government involvement is similar to that followed in the United Kingdom, France, and Austria—whereas Egypt now seeks to move away from a kind of centralized control resembling that of the USSR.

In both countries, the government role is considerably greater than establishing and maintaining the rules of the game and applying conventional indirect controls to guide the economy in the desired directions. But socialism of the usual textbook variety does not exist in either country. Both economies have big problems stemming from their several wars, but in no sense are the wars the only source of difficulty. For Israel, the problem of establishing a new nation with a culture, tradition, and outlook different from those prevailing elsewhere in the region has been paramount. In many ways, Egypt is underdeveloped, and yet despite its involvement in a series of wars, it achieved its revolutionary goals in the early 1950s and successfully restructured its revolution in the early 1970s. Both events affected all aspects of Egyptian society. Even without wars and large military outlays, the tasks facing it were enormous.

In any effort to appraise the policies followed by the Egyptian and Israeli governments, it is simply essential to keep in mind the complexity, subtlety, and deep-rootedness of the problems of economic management on both sides. The same is true of attempts, such as this one, to suggest new policies and possibilities for cooperation.

Problems and Obstacles

Six specific problem areas seem most relevant to the question of cooperation between Israel and Egypt.

Economic Distortions

In both countries, policies designed to shield the population from the high cost of military preparedness have led to considerable distortion in the use of resources. This is especially true in Egypt, where controls have been employed to the extent that market prices often bear little relation to real costs or to demand. Yet it is exceedingly difficult to raise current prices. Egyptian cotton production and the Egyptian textile industry illustrate the nature of this problem.

Under present arrangements the land area to be devoted to cotton production is determined by the government. Each farmer in the cotton-growing areas is required to devote a specified portion of his land to cotton. The farmer then sells all his cotton to the government at a price it sets, a price currently well below the world market price. In return, the farmer gets free water, and the prices he pays for seeds, pesticides, and fertilizer are subsidized. Farmers now seek to avoid cotton wherever possible, concentrating on fruits and vegetables, which are largely free of controls, instead. Freeing cotton of controls, however, has a variety of implications. Egypt's textile industry uses domestic long-staple cotton, which it buys at prices below world prices. If the textile industry had to pay world prices for Egyptian raw cotton, it could not survive without raising its prices and securing greater market protection. Raising textile prices, however, would have harmful consequences for efforts to protect low-income groups; it would reduce domestic demand and weaken the ability of the Egyptian textile industry to compete in the world market. While controls remain in effect, consumption of raw cotton by the Egyptian textile industry continues to increase. Cotton available for export is thus reduced. Moreover, the amount of land available for raising cotton declines as population increases. There is no simple way out of this complex problem. Although the misallocation is acknowledged, it is also recognized that simply letting prices go free would cause unacceptably severe dislocations. In the last few years some short-staple cotton has been imported for the textile mills, but the practice is open to question because harmful insects and other pests might come with the cotton.

Other examples might be adduced, but the nature of the problem is clear. To carry such heavy burdens for so long, Egypt has had to establish increasingly comprehensive controls and centralized decisionmaking. The controls have become less effective as the control instruments have grown weaker and as the economy has become more and more distorted. Perhaps the single most fundamental problem that Egypt faces in the next few years is to effect a transition to a more open, more decentralized, more market-oriented system in which both the private and public sector play significant roles. Any such transition involves the risk of short-run disruptions that could bring the whole process to a halt.

The distortions of the Israeli economy are almost as severe. The rate of open inflation in Israel has been greater, and inflation has induced some distortion. Price controls are extensive, and the subsidized prices of key consumer items has added greatly to the government's deficit and hence to inflationary pressure. Israel's policy of indexing wages has caused real wages and per capita consumption to rise significantly in the last few years. The policy of accepting all Jews who choose to enter Israel and to provide for them a minimum standard of living has imposed on the government a costly task that feeds inflation and complicates investment allocation. The subsidized prices of public services and products such as telephone service, rail and airline transportation, and water probably cause considerable inefficiency. Capacity utilization has apparently decreased (though measurement is difficult), and in an overheated economy underutilization represents distortion in resource allocation.

Both Israel and Egypt have pursued import substitution as a development strategy, especially in the 1950s and 1960s. This, too, has added to the difficulty of using resources efficiently. In all import substitution strategies so far invented, the chief difficulty has been to design an import policy that both protects and provides competition and the threat of competition. So it has been with Israel and Egypt. As policymakers seek a more effective use of resources, they will have to identify and take account of the dislocations and costs of dismantling the policies adopted to promote import substitution. In this respect Israel has been much more successful than Egypt.

To recapitulate: the heavy economic pressure under which each economy has existed for many years has not only resulted in the usual assortment of macroeconomic problems, but has also caused substantial misallocation of resources. Hence bottlenecks and shortages exacerbate the macroeconomic difficulties. The economies become and remain extremely vulnerable, and their vulnerability makes it harder to move the economy toward a more efficient use of resources. This problem is especially acute in Egypt, where the government has officially declared its intent to foster a more open, liberal system. And Israel will face the same problem in coping with its present severe economic difficulties. The problem for both countries would be ameliorated, though not solved, if military expenditures were significantly reduced or aid significantly increased. It is worth noting that the gap between Israel's imports and exports is about equal to its defense outlays.

The Conduct of Macroeconomic Policy

As just noted, managing an economy under great pressure is made much more difficult by the existence of severe distortions. Indeed, when distortions are severe, the line between macroeconomics and microeconomics is even fuzzier than it usually is. A clearer understanding of how to control aggregate demand in the two countries would help greatly, particularly because neither in Egypt nor in Israel are indirect instruments—such as interest rates, tax policy, and open market operations—very efficacious.

Direct taxes yield about 20 percent of government revenue in Egypt and 35–40 percent in Israel. Government deficits in both countries are financed almost entirely by direct borrowing from central banks. Private investment is largely controlled through licenses and credit allocations. Private consumption is affected by tax rates in Israel, but in Egypt the use of direct taxes to affect the level of private consumption is in its infancy. Thus, the instruments available to policymakers in both countries for controlling aggregate demand do not appear potent enough for the tasks at hand.

For these reasons, the twin tasks of eliminating distortions and controlling aggregate demand will continue to challenge policymakers in both countries.

Maintaining and Replacing Capital Stock

In many economies under siege for extended periods, the choice between maintaining existing plant and equipment or replacing it becomes agonizing. Especially in Egypt, existing capital stock is allowed to deteriorate while new capital is added. This happens partly because some aid funds must be used in a particular way, but also because maintenance can often be postponed in expectation of better days. Without proper maintenance, capital stock becomes less and less productive and eventually complete renovation is necessary. Deferred maintenance has created acute housing problems in both countries, and in Egypt the quality of the land has deteriorated because expenditures needed to preserve it have been slighted.

The general problem here is that of allocating investable resources wisely. The body of written material dealing with it has little to say on capital maintenance, which, in many practical situations, is a particularly complex question. In Israel much of the capital stock is of more recent origin than in Egypt, and the maintenance problem may be less extensive. In certain sectors, however, such as housing, the maintenance problem is acute. The high rate of inflation in Israel seems to have diverted investment funds from productive activities to speculation in such things as real estate.

Productivity

Any increase or decline in labor productivity in Israel or Egypt directly affects inflation policy, wage and employment policy, income distribution policy, and output. Productivity is thus a key variable to focus on in assessing the performance of both economies before and after a peace treaty is concluded.

In general, labor productivity in Israel is much higher than in Egypt, largely because of more capital stock per worker and a more experienced, better trained labor force. For these reasons, Israel has found it possible to apply more productive technology than Egypt can. In Israel, productivity has grown slowly in recent years, however, and the contribution to productivity growth from immigration is declining as the rate of immigration declines. The declining rate of investment also suggests that future rates of productivity increase will not be high. In Egypt, productivity growth measurement (and definition) is made complex by lack of data on employment and output. It is sometimes difficult to distinguish between true employment and nominal employment that really is a means of effecting transfer payments. Egyptian productivity is low, however measured, and finding ways to increase it is essential to the relief of Egypt's problems.

Distribution of Income and Employment

Income seems to be more evenly distributed in Israel than in Egypt: the richest 10 or 20 percent receive a smaller proportion of total income than in Egypt, partly by virtue of very high marginal tax rates and modest property income. Some reports, however, show that Israeli tax laws have been less vigorously enforced in recent years than they were previously and that continued inflation has interfered with the government's income distribution objective because indexation is not (and cannot be) complete. Israeli government services probably reach a large proportion of the lower income groups.

Income distribution data for Egypt are less satisfactory and more out of date. The Egyptian revolution of 1952 had an important equalizing effect on income distribution, especially by virtue of land reform programs. To a lesser extent the nationalizations of the early 1960s did also. It seems very probable that income distribution has become somewhat more uneven in recent years, and hence the government has attached more importance to controlling the prices of consumer goods, subsidizing housing, and so on. The availability of certain government-supplied services such as housing has not kept pace with population growth.

In both countries income distribution is a live political issue, owing partly to long years of deprivation. Even in Israel, where per-capita consumption is higher than it is in most of the rest of the world, decontrolling prices of items consumed by lower income groups creates considerable anxiety. The distribution of income in Israel has become a more controversial issue as the non-Jewish population increases and the skill and experience of immigrants decline. The task in both countries is to ensure that inequality in the distribution of income (or burdens) associated with the resolution of other problems does not create further economic and social problems.

Employment is closely linked to income distribution. Employment in Egypt, especially government employment, is often a means of effecting transfer payments. It is hardly a satisfactory means, but the absence of productive employment opportunities makes change difficult. The severe limitation on land, the rapid rate of growth of the labor force, the difficulty of maintaining a high rate of investment, and the outflow of skilled and experienced workers all contribute to making employment a complex problem indeed in Egypt. It is made yet more difficult by the urgency of other demands such as the need to improve the country's economic infrastructure, to replace capital stock, to increase foreign exchange earnings, to develop new industries and new technologies, to increase output, and to develop land. Evidence from several countries suggests that large amounts of capital are more easily raised and more quickly spent if used to build "things" and if less tangible or immediate objectives (especially employment and distribution objectives) are subordinated.

Employment objectives in Israel are somewhat less complex, but in recent years employment growth has been heavily concentrated in public services and financial services. Employment in other sectors has increased only at very modest rates even as output has increased rapidly. This may be evidence that labor was hoarded during a preceding downturn in activity, but it may also hint at difficulties of absorbing new immigrants into the Israeli economy. As the government bureaucracy increases, evidence of underutilized labor among civil servants also increases, while some private sector firms complain of a labor shortage.

Long-Run Development Strategy

A long-run strategy of economic development is difficult to define and pursue in the best of circumstances. In the midst of continuing, multifaceted crises, it is virtually impossible. In any country, the immediately urgent, if ultimately subordinate, matters will be treated before those whose much greater importance will become evident only after the passage of time.

President Sadat's October Paper of 1973, a remarkably powerful statement, advocated opening up the Egyptian economy and increasing reliance on market forces. Its general arguments apparently emerged from Sadat's conclusion that a continuation of the economic management techniques and ideas inherited from Nasser simply were no longer workable. Sadat also concluded that Egypt's links with the USSR were risky and that technology from the West and money from the Arab oil world could be combined with Egyptian labor in an especially fruitful way. All this implied that a more open, more market-oriented system was necessary. Since the October paper was issued, the foreign investment law (Law 43), and its revision have been promulgated, but a set of policies that give specific content to the general philosophy presented in the October paper has not evolved so far. There are two main reasons for this. First, the October paper reflected a genuine change in Egypt's approach to economic development and to economic policymaking. For the preceding twenty years, underlying government policy had been quite different. Government machinery had become adapted to the earlier policy, and civil servants had developed attitudes and practices consistent with it. Thus the general economic and social environment must be changed to accommodate a new and markedly different approach to economic policymaking. In such circumstances change is necessarily slow.

The second reason is quite simply the enormous difficulty of the task. Just defining a strategy, for any country, intended to reverse long-established practices without creating intolerable disturbances and short-run dislocations is extremely difficult. The complexity and delicacy of the problem becomes enormously greater if the economy in question has been under the sort of pressure to which Egypt has been subjected over a long period. Moreover, Egypt lacks effective institutional arrangements for macroeconomic policymaking, even though the liberalization process is under way and changes are being made. All this suggests that great care must be taken, cautious experiments made, risks taken, and plenty of time allowed for any new strategy to be worked out and put into effect.

In Israel the problems of economic management and strategy are at once more conventional and more difficult. The chief difficulty is that of finding a way to create an economy and a society that is at home in the Middle East, yet able to exploit the advantages accruing to it as a consequence of its Western origins and influences. The design of such a strategy must reflect more than economic factors, though they are highly relevant. Internal strains may increase if the population becomes increasingly Arab and decreasingly Western.

Israel shares with many other countries right now an acute need for a management strategy to fight inflation. As already noted, Israeli inflation is severe by any criterion, and the country suffers from the lack of a well-defined strategy and management techniques to deal with it.

Finally, in both Egypt and Israel government bureaucracy hampers the design and implementation of broad strategy and specific policies.

General Prospects and Portents

It would of course be helpful to spell out in some detail the effect that peace between Israel and Egypt will have on the array of problems just discussed. This is clearly impossible, but the following remarks, which dwell mostly on what cannot be expected, may help to illuminate the issues.

There is no reason to expect a marked reduction in military expenditure. Israel's move out of the Sinai will necessitate large expenditures for military facilities elsewhere. Egypt is also eager to reequip its forces with more advanced weapons. Indeed, it is likely that military outlays will increase in both countries in the first few years after the signing of a peace treaty. No amount of aid can relieve the two countries of this burden entirely. Aid cannot substitute for the energy, the initiatives, or the time of leaders and others that must be devoted to military affairs. Hence the pressure on either economy from this source is not likely to be reduced.

It may also be that certain dormant or controlled internal tensions become more overt with peace. War or the possibility of war can (though it does not always) supply a unifying force and a willingness to accept sacrifice that tends to disappear when peace seems to be at hand. Expectations, especially after long deprivation, can quickly become unrealistic. Tensions among different groups—whether separated by income, religion, geography, or language—held in check by the recognition of a common adversary may no longer be restrained when peace comes. Some of the problems noted above—inflation and maldistribution of income especially—may become even more acute and the burdens of leadership heavier. War will no longer be an excuse for failing to resolve some of the economic problems facing the two countries.

The peace treaty will represent the acceptance of the Israeli state by Egypt, and will legitimize a role for Israel in the Middle East. The extent to which Israel can play such a role will affect the permanence and genuineness of the peace. The form that cooperation takes may be important in establishing Israel as an integral part of the region. Cooperation thus imposes the task of demonstrating to other Middle Eastern countries not merely the possibility, but indeed the profitability, of accepting Israel as a member of the Middle Eastern community of nations.

Peace will probably not lessen military claims on resources in, say, the next five years. It may also make observable and acceptable economic improvements more urgently necessary. Certain social questions may emerge as more urgent in peace than in war. Hence the demand for economic and social change may be greater while military expenditures remain extremely high. Peace may bring new problems more complex and more demanding than those of war.

Egypt and Israel have never had economic relations with each other. The formal recognition of each by the other will not represent the reestablishment of previous trade or cooperative agreements. All forms of cooperation and contact will have to start from scratch. It is therefore useful to make a few general observations before turning to some specific possibilities.

The emphasis belongs on cooperation, in contrast to aid. Although Israel has technology, management skills, and marketing capacity that Egypt lacks, and although Israel's aid programs in other parts of Africa have had a degree of success, expectations of *mutual* gain and *equal* effort seem likely to be rewarded in the present case. This seems especially so at the outset, when confidence, trust, and rapport are starting to develop. It clearly seems more advantageous and more conducive to success if the areas of cooperation are chosen so that neither Israel nor Egypt assumes an explicitly superior or managerial role and the other a subordinate or learning role. For this reason, areas of cooperation in which each country could offer something valued by the other should be sought from the beginning.

This argument calls into question the desirability of joint ventures in manufacturing in which the Egyptians supply the labor and the Israelis the technology and management skills. Such arrangements entail great risk that one nation or the other will occupy a position of dominance or control or superiority. Joint ventures are difficult enough in the best of circumstances, but joint ventures undertaken by nationals of countries that have long been at war with one another and that have very different heritages and different social organizations could well present overwhelming problems. The question of location itself is complex. A factory in Israel with an Egyptian labor force or one in Egypt with Israeli resident technicians offers many opportunities for misunderstandings and suspicion.

Similar doubts must be expressed about projects that give one country an unusual advantage over another. Perhaps the most obvious example of such a project is that of moving water from the Nile under the Suez Canal into the Sinai for eventual sharing with Israel. Economics apart, the creation of a situation in which one country can monopolize a highly strategic commodity makes the other country highly vulnerable. At least at the outset, such a project is inappropriate.

A similar argument applies to enormously complex and highly sophisticated ventures, such as the construction of a nuclear power plant located so that the power it generates could be used in both countries. This kind of project—long in building, complex and dangerous in operation—also has dubious advantages and offers opportunities for mistakes or for dominance by one country that could harm, rather than nourish, the beginnings of cooperation.

The extent to which trade between the two countries might develop is difficult to predict. Trade among Middle Eastern countries has never been large. Egypt already exports a sizeable amount of oil to Israel, but current levels of imports and exports of other commodities by Egypt and Israel do not suggest that a wide range of products would be traded as soon as a peace treaty is signed. Yet certain complementarities may well evolve. For example, Egypt may have advantages in exporting certain agricultural products that use a great deal of water or that require a more southern climate, while Israel might export products whose production requires more complex agricultural technology. Good land routes between Israel and Egypt may also result in some diversion of each country's trade with third countries to trade with each other. It is fair to conclude that trade prospects are good, but it may take some time to realize them fully.

Specific Possibilities for Cooperation

Artificial and forced forms of cooperation will not contribute to the solution of either country's problems or to the establishment of a basis for continued cooperation. Ways must be found to allow cooperation to emerge in places and in activities that are clearly to the advantage of both countries and that do not constitute a threat to either country. And the results should be clearly attributable to the cooperation.

If these generalities are well founded, it seems that cooperation would be feasible and mutually profitable in several specific areas that are important in themselves and also important as illustrations of the kind of activity or endeavor likely to be conducive to further cooperation. The suggestions made here cannot be considered blueprints for action, and it is obvious that more detailed studies are necessary before any of them could be implemented. Major hurdles and uncertainties afflict all of them. Presumably, a number of other areas will emerge as further studies are undertaken.

Information Sharing

The exchange of ideas and visits and the organization of meetings and seminars for Israelis and Egyptians can be useful in promoting cooperation of various kinds. Perhaps the most promising opportunities for such contacts are to be found in agronomy and agriculture.

Agricultural development is essential if Egypt is to establish a basis for sustained growth; it is only slightly less important for Israel. Farmers in both countries have talents and capacities that can be profitably shared and developed. Agricultural cooperation may take several forms. Visits by the farmers of each country to the other are a simple and productive form of exchange. Extended stays by some farmers especially talented in explaining, suggesting, and analyzing their work are also possible. Other areas in which exchanges could be mutually beneficial include water use, soil enrichment and preservation, fertilizer use, seed development, and farm machinery design and construction. Israel's experience in the West Bank, where yields and farm income have increased considerably, may be especially relevant. Some sharing of ideas on export marketing would also be helpful if the governments continue to relax the controls on private exporting.

Experience elsewhere suggests that local adaptive research can increase yields at low cost. The research must be local in order to take into account regional peculiarities of soil, climate, pests, labor supply, and so on. The objective of such cooperation would be not only to share what is already known, but also to accumulate new knowledge—that is, to promote local adaptation.

Similar reasoning may be applied to small-scale manufacturing activities. Increased industrial activity is of course part of the way out of the difficulties of both countries. Both countries have a large number of small-scale manufacturing units (each with fewer than, say, twenty-five employees) that already play an important role and that could play an expanded role. As in agriculture, many of these activities reflect considerable ingenuity and expertise on the part of their owners and workers. They also face many problems, and they need access to new management ideas, technologies, marketing techniques, and funds. In some instances the policies they have followed have penalized their performance. A common set of problems does not necessarily imply a common set of answers, but, it does suggest—as in agriculture—that experienced, fully involved people may profit from visits with each other and from arrangements that allow for continuing exchange of ideas.

Problems of technology and labor supply afflict most small-scale economic activity. The furniture industry, an important one in Egypt, though of lesser importance in Israel, exemplifies the issues reviewed here. In Egypt, according to an unpublished survey by Donald Mead, furniture manufacturing employs about 35,000 people in small-scale activities— units with fewer than ten workers—that supply a great range of products, from the very simple to the very sophisticated. Production techniques involve much less capital and power per worker than large-scale activities. Some power-driven machines are shared. Skilled workers and apprentices dominate the labor force; very few workers are unskilled. Almost all skills are acquired through apprenticeship and experience. Wage rates are well above average in the economy for both skilled workers and apprentices, and have been rising for both categories at a rate above the rate of inflation in recent years. The real wages of apprentices have risen especially rapidly. Despite all this, Mead's data show that furniture manufacturing suffers from lack of labor. Young people are apparently unwilling to become apprentices, preferring instead to attend school and university even though job opportunities for college graduates are less rewarding in general than those for furniture-making apprentices. Also, skilled workers are being lured away to the much higher-paying jobs in the Persian Gulf area.

Here, then, is an important activity that faces difficult problems, as do other similar activities in both countries. It seems that continuous contact between people involved in such activities in the two countries could be profitable to both. Attempts to encourage technological development and innovation in small-scale activities are likely to be richly rewarded. Such attempts are also an effort to which citizens of both countries have much to contribute. One way to make apprenticeships more attractive is to make the technology involved more exciting, without making it more capital intensive or requiring expensive formal training programs. The United States can play a useful role in this activity as well as in agriculture —a role to which attention is directed below.

Another matter of great concern to both countries is the present state and future role of government-owned or -controlled companies. In both Egypt and Israel such companies dominate the large-scale manufacturing sector, and their efficiency could be substantially increased. Greater efficiency in government enterprise is important to the development of more open, market-oriented forms of economic organization and to attracting new foreign investment. Continued withholding of new investments from government enterprises will impede the process of attracting foreign investment. Note that the issue ought to be greater efficiency, not private versus public ownership. Of course, the efficiency of government enterprises has political implications that may be too complex to permit any sort of cooperation.

Cooperation in this area is probably more difficult than in agricultural development or small-scale manufacturing activity, but the potential for mutual benefit is as great. Both governments have considerable investments in textile manufacturing, and there may be many opportunities for sharing information and technical knowledge. For example, replacement and maintenance policy in government enterprises—especially in those which appear to be inevitably uneconomic—is a problem common to both countries, as is the development and application of new technology in the circumstances that have been described. Other large-scale manufacturing activities (fertilizers, for example) may also be candidates for consultation and information sharing.

These forms of cooperation seem promising because improved technology, improved organization, and better management emerge, to a considerable degree, from numerous small modifications and slight adaptations. A great variety of such changes originate in the insights and experience of those actually engaged in the operation of an enterprise. To take advantage of this fact, incentives, organization, and social arrangements should encourage and induce a conscious search and an awareness of the rewards of increased efficiency. Conversations, seminars, and visits by the people affected can contribute to the achievement of these objectives.

For this kind of cooperation, only very modest organizing at the center would be necessary, and very little money is required. The essence of the approach is to take advantage of latent knowledge and capacity possessed by the economic agents directly concerned. It is therefore crucial to the success of the effort that it be organized and run at the lowest possible local level.

Research and Development

The establishment and conduct of formal research and development activities constitute another opportunity for cooperation of great potential advantage to both countries. Research institutes are common in many developing countries. The results of their labors are generally unimpressive, but there are notable exceptions. A number of small, low-key research institutes in various geographical areas, with research attention directed to problems specific to that locality, are likely to be more successful than a single large research factory with Egyptians and Israelis in residence.

To the extent possible, the research conducted in these institutes should be in response to questions and problems brought to it by the people in the area. The existence of a problem-solving unit, plus the accumulation of a success record, can be expected to elicit further questions from the local population. A large research institute in a central city is less likely to elicit such questions; hence it is not likely to produce much knowledge that has much relevance to the problems with which people in the field are wrestling. Meetings and discussions at small decentralized institutes may in fact generate questions that should be investigated by formal procedures in central institutions, but local research personnel can identify problems and define the specific questions on which research is needed.

The research units envisioned here would include personnel from Israel and Egypt, from other countries of the Middle East, and possibly elsewhere. The idea would be to have several small groups of people with considerable experience and some formal training who can commit themselves to this kind of endeavor.

The U.S. role in these institutes would consist of some funding, supplying of equipment, and possibly some personnel. Too much funding, too much equipment, and too many people can easily have negative effects. This kind of research-and-development activity could deal with many issues of great interest to both countries. One is the development of agricultural implements well adapted to the regions. Both countries depend heavily on irrigation and intensive land use; agricultural machinery that speeds planting and harvesting can greatly increase output. The development of new lands in both countries also seems to call for rather special equipment. A small machine to move and control water would have great utility, as would means of irrigation that reduce loss of water through evaporation or otherwise. Other promising research topics include seed development and the development of power tools usable in very small-scale enterprises. There is no lack of such topics—the real task is to orient the activity so that it yields results directly relevant to the problems facing farmers, manufacturers, poultry raisers, and all the others who make up the heart and muscle of both economies.

A somewhat more ambitious and longer-range research effort would be one concerned with developing new and cheaper ways to remove salt from seawater and more effective ways to capture energy from the sun. Such long-range research projects should be distinguished from those aiming at immediate results. For example, small plants that can reduce the brackishness of available water so that it can be used to irrigate certain forage crops even if it remains unfit for human consumption might become possible fairly soon with a concentrated research effort. Israel has done some work on such plants and Egypt has begun to explore possibilities.

Health and Medicine

Cooperation on the terms mentioned above seems likely to pay off in health-related ways: medical and hospital care, medical research in areas of common interest (tropical diseases, chronic degenerative diseases, respiratory problems, etc.), nutritional problems among low-income people, and health problems that seem linked to environmental conditions. Both countries have people well equipped to study these and other health problems. The similarity of climate and general atmosphere makes many health and medical issues common to both countries.

Two general research areas may be identified. The first—disease control, prevention, and cure—can best be conducted in well-equipped medical centers by well-trained staff. The work must be done in the region. It would not do to send Egyptians and Israelis to Europe or the United States for such research and training. The medical research centers that now exist in both countries could be strengthened in a variety of ways, and exchanges of personnel between Egyptian and Israeli institutions can be arranged. Again, the idea is to seek to take advantage of informal channels as the instrument of cooperation, and in so doing bring about an exchange of information that may lead to further understanding and control of diseases.

The second area concerns what might be called rural delivery systems. It is of interest to both countries, though more directly relevant to Egypt. The general problem is that in rural areas of most poor countries, medical services of all kinds are difficult and expensive to render. Yet such areas are afflicted with a great variety of health deficiencies, some of which require only modest medical assistance. The tasks of supplying, fostering understanding of, and creating demand for paramedical services all lend themselves to cooperation and exchange of ideas and people.

Education

Somewhat similar ideas apply to education. As already noted, Egyptians have long served as teachers in the Arabian peninsula, but there is great need for improved educational programs in Egypt at both the elementary and adult levels. Israeli needs are especially acute at the adult level as new immigrants arrive with unusable skills or none at all. Improved methods of short-term training in specific skills, such as typing and other clerical work, all categories of construction work, literacy, tool operation, and so on would be especially helpful. These kinds of educational programs can often be carried out most effectively in small institutions devoted to a single category of training. They, like the small-scale research activities, should be devoted to meeting specific, observed needs. "Crash programs" imply once-and-for-all efforts. The idea here is for the two countries to compare notes and insights and suggestions on the development of educational programs and institutions that can turn out in a matter of a few months people who can perform (or people who at least can learn to perform) essentially simple tasks, but tasks that are highly strategic at a given stage of economic development. Exchange of faculty and students would also be profitable.

Tourism

Although the value of joint ventures and bilateral trade agreements as potential areas of cooperation was questioned above (see pages 19–20), common arrangements may well be profitable to both countries in some activities, of which perhaps the most obvious is tourism. Both countries offer much in the way of historical and religious monuments. They also offer virtually unlimited sunshine, sand, and seacoast. All these attract tourists. Tourism is usually regarded as a good source of foreign-exchange earnings and as a source of employment. Increasingly, these attributes of tourism are being questioned, but most observers accept the notion that tourism could be useful in both respects under appropriate management and policy. Increasingly also, certain costs of tourism are being identified—for example, its effects on consumption and expectations; the appearance of shops, restaurants, and leisure activities that appeal mainly to the rich; and the tendency to violate or offend national values and traditions—that considerably reduce the net contribution that tourism makes to social welfare. Hence cooperation should seek not merely to increase gross revenue from tourism, but also to lower the social costs that seem to be associated with a large and steady flow of visitors.

Some form of cooperation on tours may be useful, but this should come about without explicit government action once relations between Egypt and Israel are fully opened. More important would be cooperation in the development of tourist infrastructure in areas that include both countries.

Examples are the Aqaba, Eilat, and Sharm-al-Sheikh areas. If these were developed as tourist regions, cooperation on water, power, sewage, and transportation is likely to be advantageous. Such infrastructure investment might be shared in other regions as well.

One possible way of reducing the social-welfare costs of tourism is to locate tourist centers apart from large urban areas. Since many tourists come to both countries to sun themselves on beaches, various locations away from big cities can be chosen. At any rate, the cooperative exploration of tourist development—with social and economic costs under scrutiny as well as revenue—is another activity that may yield considerable mutual benefit.

A few other activities may offer similar opportunities for cooperation, among them transportation and perhaps banking. Unfortunately, it does not seem that the list would be very long.

Environmental Quality

Another area in which the prospects for successful cooperation seem to be especially good is environmental quality—the control of air and water pollution in particular. Some developing countries ignore the issue on the ground that pollution control is a luxury they can ill afford. This is questionable, and in certain locations cooperation between or among countries may be necessary if any program is to be at all effective.

Workable methods of pollution control are difficult to establish, and no approach or set of approaches is both available and efficacious. Cooperation in this endeavor would take the form of establishing links between the control instruments used in the two countries. The general issue of pollution includes a range of specific issues (such as fishing practices, sewage disposal, fertilizing procedures, factory siting practices, and forestation techniques, for example) that require international cooperation if they are to be dealt with in a satisfactory manner.

Land Development and Preservation

Both Israel and Egypt have a large stake in the development of "new" lands—lands not now cultivated or inhabited. Citizens of both countries have learned a great deal about this enormous task in recent years. Many issues are involved—soil improvement, water use, salinity, and fertilization, among others—and evidence to date suggests that the problem is enormously complex and costly. Recent increases in the cost of energy have cast further doubts on the wisdom of developing new lands. Yet it is such a crucial question, both economically and politically, that further studies are necessary. And it is much too complex to be left to the kind of cooperative seminars and research-and-development activities described above.

The exact form that the cooperation should take in developing new lands is not clear. Studies and the design of policies and techniques should be undertaken by nationals of both countries in an effort to exchange as many insights and as much experience as possible. Pilot projects are likely to be especially useful because available technical knowledge is so skimpy and region-specific and because costs are so very high. The United States can play a financing role here and possibly supply technical experts to work with their Israeli and Egyptian counterparts.

In Egypt and Israel, land development refers not only to turning desert lands into agriculturally productive lands, but also to making desert lands available for new settlements and towns. For the latter purpose, soil quality is less important than other matters such as water purity, power, and sewage disposal.

The development of new lands is a long-term process in Egypt, as elsewhere. It appears possible, however, to show evidence of progress by concentrating efforts on small areas and demonstrating that the whole idea makes sense technically and economically.

OTHER activities could doubtless be identified as suitable for cooperative endeavor. As noted earlier, the listing here is meant merely to call attention to, rather than to explore in detail, the kinds of activity in which cooperation seems possible as well as the forms of cooperation that seem appropriate. Much more study is likely to be needed before cooperative action can actually begin.

Conclusion

The achievement of true peace between Egypt and Israel will be one of the great events of recent decades. Many years marked by war and the threat of war have imposed great burdens on both populations and entrenched distrust on both sides. With such a history, cooperation between the Egyptian and Israeli people and their governments can proceed but slowly. This paper has sought to emphasize cooperative efforts where opportunities for mutual profit appeared greatest and where citizens of both countries could contribute in a significant way. Pushing cooperation hard for the sake of cooperation alone will surely fail. It is cooperation for problem-solving that is at the heart of the matter, and patience should be the watchword.

THE BROOKINGS INSTITUTION

Washington, D.C.

ISBN 0-8157-1125-5